GUIDING CLIENTS THROUGH RETIREMENT

GUIDING CLIENTS THROUGH RETIREMENT

B. VINCENT

CONTENTS

CHAPTER 1

Introduction

One of the happiest moments in individuals' lives comes with the decision to retire, explains Preet Banerjee, consultant, mentor, and lecturer in behavioural finance. "Retirees are euphoric; why shouldn't they be when they have worked hard to amass a nest egg that will fund the rest of their lives?" he asks. Mr. Banerjee will be guiding advisors through life after work at The Investment Funds Institute of Canada's (IFIC) Strategic Forum, 2013 in Toronto on November 19th. This column offers a preview of his presentation.

In a world with sequelsful job turnover, "asset sales" during the "Neanderthal days of wealth management," and unretirement, assisting people into retirement can be valuable "and generates a lot of long-term revenue," Mr. Banerjee says. For advisors, this is an opportunity to develop "a great exit strategy" with the form, which could be a career juncture, a value add on when they are looking for a successor, or a business plan. "Frankly, I don't care how they price it or what they call it. All I care about is that they have a business set up that grows when their client is taking money out of their portfolio," he explains. After the financial advising industry in the United States tackled transitions such as those from commission to satellite advisors, from sole proprietors to RIA firms, and from product sales to asset management, a most recent one – exit strategy – is "setting advisors off in families," Mr. Banerjee says. "'We'll give you access to this and you give us access to that,' kind of thing," he says. The tendency could work up into larger branches' transition, within the same firm, as advisors hand over books of business to a younger advisor.

CHAPTER 2

Understanding Retirement Planning

Before understanding the need for classic retirement planning, it's important to grasp the terminology and the concepts associated with this important process. The Employee Retirement Income Securities Act of 1974 (ERISA) remains the quintessential foundation of retirement planning. That regulation, in addition to 29 code 401 through 419, created traditional retirement planning as we know it. ERISA was designed to provide increased protection of pension and employee welfare benefits to participants and beneficiaries in private sector employee benefit programs. This legislation is very similar to the Social Security Act of 1935 that provided defined benefit guaranteed lifetime income plans for many of the US citizens.

The definition of retirement is to discontinue work and exhibit leisure behavior. The absence or presence of work is a poor definition of retirement. Also, the true set of retirement should be the analysis through death, but no one plans that far into the future. Additional vocabularies that should spark some interest are mortality, ethnicity, career history, voluntary work, unintentional work, forced work, social capital, capital markets, false expectations, longevity, and health risks.

What follows is an insight into the key elements of retirement in America. However, the reader should know that not all elements are agreed upon. The Income Generation, reported in an article that appeared in the Retirement Management, states this about Americans: "retirement readiness is a vital issue that spans a broad range of related topics, including factors that predict retirement and wealth, the numerous puzzles surrounding the Social Security and Medicare systems, and options and alternatives for funding retirement."

Key Concepts and Terminology

Even if retirement is years away for your clients, it's never too early to start laying the groundwork of preparation with them. Assets and experiences they have today will begin contributing to a successful search for their exit strategy. By identifying clients who are making or have made plans for a new chapter in life, your firm can assist with a smooth departure.

To begin, clients may use assets accumulated while working to educate themselves, either in groups or workshops or one-on-one counseling. Finances should be a disciplined focus to plan and execute a successful exit; however, retirement may outline a time lifestyle will change. Educational products include group workshops offered once or several times a year, weekly in-depth sessions for an individual who will be offered during alternative times, training for agents, and marketing tools and follow up with referrals to needed services.

Retirement: ending one's work and withdrawing from one's occupation, business, or office, usually because of age: also, withdrawal into seclusion or privacy focusing on leisure. Those making the (approximately) 10-year transition to retirement, that segment named pre-retirement. That which is for new retirees. In this site, we interchangeably discuss experiences related to these three documented periods. (What is retirement?) From pre-retirement to retirement. This paper takes an alternative approach by looking at the time at which pre-retirement morphs into retirement. This is around age 68.65 in Europe. Given a period of work with the same employer, it began at Xt using on-the-job training. It ended after Zt+10 years. What is a responsible time to end training? We use our estimates to construct a normative guide. This considers not only when to stop training, but also whether to invest and how retirement is affected.

Types of Retirement Accounts

The main types of retirement accounts include:

Individual Retirement Accounts (IRA): IRA accounts are set up at a bank or a brokerage and can hold various types of investments including stocks, bonds, mutual funds, ETFs, and CDs. IRAs can be broken into two categories - Traditional and Roth. There are different tax treatments and regulations for each type of account. IRA holders can contribute up to $6,000/year if they are under 50 and up to $7,000/year if they are over 50. The amount contributed can be offset by contributions to 401ks, however. Early withdrawal penalties are levied for most accounts.

Simplified Employee Pension-Individual Retirement Account (SEP IRAs): SEP IRAs are designed to allow small business owners a tax-deferred way to save for their retirement. This account is established by the employer on behalf of the employee. This is a type of traditional IRA to which the employer makes contributions. The maximum contribution the employer is allowed to make to the SEP IRA account is the lesser of 25% of employee compensation or $61,000 for 2022. Unlike a traditional IRA, where the account holder makes tax-deductible contributions, the employer, not the employee, is the one who makes the contribution to the plan. Withdrawals are taxed as ordinary income. Early withdrawals are possible, but subject to a 10% penalty.

Social Security and Medicare

From decimating the workforce to the current transient labor force to its effect on investment markets, the baby boomers' retirement impacts a variety of professions, means of employment, and professions. From your own personal finance perspective, this section on Social Security and Medicare aims to provide a better understanding of these two massive and complicated systems to help you grasp potential future vulnerabilities. Many personal financial strategies revolve around when to initiate them. Having a fuller insight into how they are planned or how they are affected by other funding such as Social Security or pensions might also decide between trade-offs and other personal financial issues. Within the battles over Medicare funding, the duo has also been presented as one potential option for cutting considerably through income-streaming alone. It also looks at the basics of Medicare planning for easy descriptions, previous research, and links to the Social Security site for complete explanations.

On some pieces of this, a little tune-up would have been made possible and referred to changes after the end of this publication from the SSA or Medicare sites. The planning for retirement and estate fees in Medicare is an intricate act that touches certain aspects of personal finance. The nature of Medicare has also replaced much of the planning with recent Medicare reform. This section aims to combine research and theory on Medicare. Medicare is composed of two different parts that act in very different ways and have comprehensive planning implications. Elect to enjoy medical insurance, Medicare Part B, including doctor and outpatient care. If you don't see to since you have current workplace insurance, fines, and your Social Security benefits paid for a physician, you might ignore Part B.

CHAPTER 3

Client-Centered Approach

Topic: Guiding Clients Through Retirement: Tools for a Smooth Exit and Group Referrals Client-Centered Approach. Our clients' aspirations and fears drive all that we do. Consequently, our first step is to address, not just our members' goals, but also their records, financial plan, financial resale value, and the trustworthiness of investment media.

In our first meetings with our retirees, we use the usual financial planning sources of information. We meet with our clients face-to-face in a quiet location, including our conference room or the retiree's/active worker's living room. We do not hurry through this process because we need time to make our clients feel comfortable enough to share their experiences and information with us. We do not want someone to focus on some earlier hurt and think we are just after their dollar. We let them tell us their "story." Unfortunately, the breakthrough successes, as well as the near misses, are of equal informative value on many retirement statuses. If someone cannot get past a work situation long enough to provide the valuable pre-retirement information, we refer them to someone else.

We gather information on our members' family status and health status, as well as their economic orientation and collect as many of their pay stubs as possible. The pay stubs, along with the W-2 information, allow us to dry how much our clients net and how much of the several mandated programs, like health insurance costs, are deducted from their paychecks and are not in our clients' take-home checkbooks.

We also ask our clients about their experiences with previous advisors. "What has been your experience with other financial advisors? What qualities have you enjoyed most in other advisors? Is there anything that you did not like about money managers or financial advisors you have worked with? What financial advisor did you fire or let go from managing your money? What did they do that so upset you? And, where would you rank money managers in the long-term viability of your success, from 1 (I must have one to be successful) to 10 (I can do this better on my own)?" These questions are designed to guide us in determining the life cycle orientation of each member.

For example, we found that the pre-WWII clients had mostly negative experiences with financial industry sales professionals. They do not like to be called on the phone or called salesman. If you could not show them how to preserve their principal, you had no business approaching this kind of client. The Baby Boomers are a bit more receptive to "thinking" about an offer, only if the member in our own words suggests the business transaction not already be an existing pre-packaged investment program. A reference point for this group is BuyDirect at Charles Schwab. The Gen-Xers like to "think" out loud, and their questions revolve around "thinking" plans of action. But just because they are feasible, easy to manage, and their deposit friend patted them on the back and said whatever you want to do is okay with me, they cannot bring themselves to "pull the trigger" on the program. It is just too good to be true to just fall into place, as do their other investment decisions.

We try to get a feel for what money means to the various retirees and potential retirees. Some like to pull it all out and keep it under the mattress. Some are oriented towards doing savings themselves. And some individuals prefer to invest in professionally managed funds where the money grows automatically. We are very careful to assess the money orientation of our own customers to ensure asset allocation strategies are chosen that are in keeping with our client needs and fears. We do not overcome the client's fear of loss and any new 5% class investments.

Assessment of Client Goals and Needs

A fundamental part of any financial plan is seeking to clearly understand the client's goals and visions for the future. This future could very well include retirement as the main goal a professional wealth manager is tasked to assist with. The starting point we use to understand a client's needs is to conduct an initial meeting where their needs can be discussed and likely agreed on. A clear understanding of what a client's personal and financial objectives allows an advisor to form a real picture of the risk options suitable to be documented in a statement of advice. It also helps ensure a tangible solution being the result of a tailored and personalized process. Some items to think about when it comes to retirement could include:

- Strategy return - Retirement goals - Assumptions and needs

For instance, all definitions of goals should include an income, as cost of living needs do not really change for anyone not traveling overseas, or significant other changes and a change in their disposable net income. Only when this common ground has been well covered should an advisor then attempt to upsell services such as additional offers like estate and aged care planning. How it differs per client group and the retirement journey. For example, discussed will be the different advice requirements of the average bloke or 'client' vs the self-managed super fund 'client'.

This is not necessarily a new concept. It has always been a consideration in the development of broad practice solutions. Plus, solution tailoring and utilization do not always occur in the legislative and cost efficiency space; it is also seen in the numerous professional indemnity insurance-related cases where a better outcome may have been achieved if any subsequent action were that of the alternate profession, such as an accountant. If identified in the early years of the journey, the possibilities for the client to reach their goals, then expectations can be set and an appropriate custom proposition built. It is best for a concepts-driven process to be used where open, unstructured questions are asked to feel out what the customer wants in retirement. Ideally, the client would be prompted to answer open-ended questions with responses that create a quantifiable financial variance. For example: What color brogues would you like to be wearing on the day of your retirement party?

Risk Tolerance and Investment Strategies

Risk tolerance and time are pivotal elements in each individual's financial plan. It is important to develop a proper understanding of client attitudes toward investments and the intended utilization of assets. A large number of tools related to these issues have been developed to try to put specific profiles onto clients and determine the appropriate encounter products. Such tools also get criticized - that they are created by the sales-oriented industry and do not generate the automatic dilution of the "plan" before going to the recommendation. The other point is that the investor can almost imagine that they will sell funds that have reached the top or market derivatives. Discommodity to such thoughts is part of our function, a reversed view, and a healthy Swiss formation to walk away. Anyone can comprehend when a market is up and just as easy to sell potential market funds.

While some might say the need for such instruments is the most used, they are unable to be denied. At least from a disciplinary point of view, they explain that the recommended investment essentially meets the investor's profile. The approach to obligations, mainly directly dependent on the required income; this is associated with necessary expenditures and desires; time is a preferred Holtgrefe; and lastly, the opportunity or suitable in compliance with. They reserve too little - living overdue happy he may last in death abundance likely not soon - and too many are compounds; Spend too much later - one life is a poverty constituent alive preschool - and balance is both now and dead in coming years. A financial advisor helps clients to participate in this fifth option as quickly as possible and then have everything on their own should control the change.

CHAPTER 4

Estate Planning and Wealth Transfer

Estate planning refers to the accumulation, conservation, and distribution of an estate in accordance with the goals of its owner. A comprehensive wealth accumulation plan will be more effective when all of the estate planning issues are addressed. Estate planning is for the living. It is an opportunity to transfer not just true property, real and personal, but intangible values from one generation to the next. Estate planning is a sound investment strategy. It is not only concerned with the person transferring the wealth; it takes into account the attitudes, educational needs, and concerns of children and grandchildren. The objective of estate planning is to provide an equitable distribution of assets to those surviving after the family head has died. It is carried out according to the wishes of the decedent as outlined in their state's probate code.

Wealth transfer is the act of moving personal or business assets from a person, couple, or business owner to other people or entities, such as other family members or charities. For many affluent clients, their primary intangible wealth is already inside their business. As a result, this most often leaves them with two primary opportunities to effectively transfer wealth to a future generation – either through the business or related real estate, or through their personal estate. Using business assets, they may transfer business ownership - both management and/or equity - to other family members, either in whole or in part, for tax-advantaged intra-family buy-out. Similarly, with personal estate assets, they may gift or leave a portion of their wealth to their beneficiaries as well. Wealth transfer planning often involves the following transfer strategies: gifting, borrowing, buying, and financing. It is important that it be done as tax efficiently as possible. That isn't merely minimizing the direct tax cost; if she or he runs into terminally slow money after wealth transfer planning has been completed, it's a fail-safe fact: programs that forget how to make wealth-generating investments are guaranteed to lose ground due to inflation.

CHAPTER 5

Tax Considerations in Retirement

A significant consideration for clients in retirement is the taxation of their assets, both from a withdrawal standpoint and from a long-term capital gains consideration.

As clients are considering when to retire, it can be beneficial to consider the tax implications of when they will withdraw from their assets. If clients are waiting to take Social Security or pension benefits, it can be beneficial to exhaust their tax-deferred dollars before taking either of these sources of income. This can increase the tax-efficiency of the pension/Social Security in the early years. In considering these withdrawal amounts, be sure to maximize the standard or itemized deduction. Additionally, it would be valuable to consider the potential taxation of Social Security when looking at the taxation of asset withdrawals. This is because the tax threshold for Social Security is based off an individual's gross income with up to 85% of Social Security being taxable. Withdrawals should only be taken to the extent of accessing the 0% long-term capital gains tax bracket or the tax threshold of Social Security, often targeting - where prudent - as little as $40,000 to $60,000 of income to avoid Medicare and Social Security taxation. After the first year or two, we can build tax-efficient distributions into the long term while we still can.

When looking at long-term accumulated assets, it is crucial to look at brackets and our long-term current change. When currently retiring in the 10-12% tax bracket, the income of 22% tax bracket is an additional $40,425 for single ($80,850 for Married Filing Jointly). Think of these thresholds in terms of withdrawals, not Roth conversions. If you have too much income going into the 22% bracket additionally, you can convert the maximum amount in the 22% tax bracket - $40,000-$60,000 of income, which will likely be above the 22% bracket.

CHAPTER 6

Healthcare and Long-Term Care Planning

Healthcare & Long-Term Care Planning: This section provides a rich source of information focusing on healthcare and long-term care. In these days, they are one of the key parts of retirement. Every one of us should know what is important and what is not for good planning in this area.

Healthcare Planning

Factors to Consider: 1. Medicare – Parts and Coverage 2. Medigap & Medicaid 3. Drug Plan Coverage – Part D PEAK 4. Income-related Premium Adjustment 5. Mail Order Drugs 6. Regional Medical Centers (Hospitals) 7. Accountable Healthcare Organizations (ACOs) 8. Impact of Health Status on Income and Spending

Dentures: What should you know with Medicare? Check-ups (examples): 1. Cardiovascular system, cholesterol, diabetes 2. Cancer screening, fast relation to your current condition 3. Is prevention better than cure? 4. Osteoporosis, Janet's story...

Long-Term Care

1. Planning for Long-Term Care Costs for Home and Assisted Living Facilities 2. Medicaid Planning 3. Determining the Risk of

Need for Long-Term Care 4. Should You Buy Long-Term Care Insurance? 5. A Medicaid Asset Protection Trust (Adams Trust)

What happens if you are incapable and cannot pay the bills any longer? Many nursing homes expect a private resident to pay for 2-4 years before applying for Medicaid. What is your plan to pay for help at home personally or in an Assisted Living Facility? Some areas over $3,000 per month and they all expect that resident paid until their assets are at a required level. Only about 4,000 people in the US have Long-Term care insurance. Should you buy Long-Term Care Insurance? Each person, based on your net worth and your family's history of long-term care, must decide if LTC insurance fits their portfolio. If you make a mistake on this one, you won't be around to see it. Some of the main features of Long-Term Care insurance are age, health, cost, benefit periods, inflationary protection, elimination period, and partial home care coverage. Also have the traditional guarantee, reimbursements, daily or monthly benefits, waived of premium, dollar benefits, and pre-existing condition waiting period. The state of Idaho provides a credit of up to $80 per year against your state income tax if you buy Long-Term Care Insurance.

CHAPTER 7

Income Planning and Withdrawal Strategies

Clients need help transitioning from a saver's mindset to a spender's mindset. Approaching the spending phase as a continuation of the accumulation phase can make this more palatable for many clients. But for some, it can create anxiety. A high level of replacement ratio will often not pass the smell test for the mathematically inclined. In addition, clients often have discretionary spending wants that could go unfulfilled if they offer every dime above target. We'll illustrate the particulars of one cohabit to assuage the concerns of a tightwad reader. While some retirees have the income to support some of these desires from their natural cash flow sources, many will need to dip into the principle of their investable assets to fulfill their desires. Share information on multiple withdrawal strategies.

The complexity for this area comes not in the decision of what to spend but in managing the portfolio to ensure the wealth will last over a long and uncertain retirement period. The client must consider: life expectancy, portfolio risk, variable spending expectations, partial spending of inheritances, multi-generational bequests, and charitable goals. To smooth income, the consideration of a reserve account for planned spending (such as annual planned share increase for long-term care cost-of-living adjustments) is often recommended. Taxes have a big effect on how much one spends if the additional income puts the client into 85% of taxable social security and 100% taxable social security range. The before and after-tax spending should be calculated in determining the amount of additional wealth to vest right now for the infusion of additional future spending. Potential qualified plan taxation should also be considered, particularly when the client has stock acquired through options.

CHAPTER 8

Utilizing Technology in Retirement Planning

Technology is transforming the financial services industry - including retirement planning. In order to efficiently do retirement planning, advisors now have access to incredibly powerful algorithms and software programs that help forecast retirement outcomes and how different financial-planning scenarios might affect that outcome. Many of those applications also have a digital or direct-to-consumer alternative, opening up the ability to create and illustrate retirement income strategies with your clients, as well as create a potential digital tool to enhance engagement with your clients and potential new clients.

There are a few reasons you might want to explore retirement-planning technology, including:

- If you're going to do a seminar on retirement assets/income and want to have prospects come into your office for a no-obligation meeting. This software can be used to give the seminar attendees a real dollar tour of their future - something that 100% of financial education retirees wish they had 100% financial literate vs. 50% of financial illiterate. It can be used to convert seminar attendees into appointments, giving one a retirement income review. - As a strong, client-facing computer tool to take clients through during a sophomore slump meeting. If you're only reviewing asset allocation or meeting investment returns in this meeting, it's highly possible that the prospective retiree might not see a reason to continue to come in for meetings. Time to retire quickly making those asset management fees unsustainable.

The role of a financial planner is to guide clients from the accumulation phase into retirement and to serve them beyond. The sixth step of retirement coaching for advisors is to make the client not just adjustable, but to make them skyrocket. When looking into a retirement planning program, remember that retirees must select portfolios that also offer guarantees. Look to make the percentages that are committed to safe investments, such as a Defined Benefit Pension plan, as high.

CHAPTER 9

Working with Group Referrals

In your work, you may come across lucrative group distributions. For example, you might meet with a teacher who aims to retire soon and who can connect you by email with the rest of the social studies department at her school. These sorts of group referrals are based on your recommendation and collegiality. Periodically, have the client you helped write an email that we'll send to others, explaining their experience, what they achieved financially, and the value of meeting with you. Have that client give us their work email list of up to 30 people in order for a smooth transition to occur upon a successful booking, becoming the advocate for gathering all of their colleagues to help them.

Leverage a group email sent by a colleague (our client) to offer financially smart speakers and meeting rooms on the premise of the employer. The email does all the heavy lifting getting people to attend and brings them to your presentation. Always arrive early to set up, should it be required. In the presentation, share how you can help people fulfill their retirement goals after creating a long-term blueprint, which goes hand-in-hand with helping them protect their interests and future quality of life. You also explain that teachers (or another group) have a hidden fee inside their 403(b) plans and show them what the fees are and why the teachers just can't "learn to live with it" once they know. For helping them this way, the teachers or other group members who are vested tend to favor rolling it out, and they're more willing to make an appointment that same day.

CHAPTER 10

Building Strategic Partnerships

By this second year, you should begin to build strategic partnerships. A list of attorneys and CPAs will be vital to you for retirement planning. A list of local and national reverse mortgage lenders may prove valuable, as among those three groups, these are excellent prospects. As you guide your clients through retirement, the team may include them at various discussions, with your client's advance permission.

Strategic partnerships have dialogue meetings at least twice a year. This year, I urge you to start getting together with the professionals just mentioned, as well as college financial aid officers, please don't forget them, and estate planning attorneys. Estate planning attorneys can get very comfortable funneling business to you once they trust you. Next month, on the first Monday, begin to meet with people who move the masses, such as hospital social workers and human services folks. The more you can make of these meetings, creating opportunities, the more successful you will be. Ask the client for the attorney's name. On your computer, go to the website of the state bar association. In the search box, ask to see if that attorney has ever been disciplined. He or she may have been disciplined when he was

35, but if he is 70 now and without further issues, this would not necessarily exclude him. Remember: statistics are on your side. If a doctor graduates from medical school, he normally practices medicine for 35 years before becoming a patient.

How can you start laying the groundwork for the ten-to-twenty year relationship between an attorney and you? First, you will need to send out a folder about yourself. This folder will include an introduction on yourself, education, books written, published articles, and a word about your firm. A fee sheet is imperative. Also, let people know that you are a problem-solver, not a product-pusher, and that the majority of your business is derived from referrals. I will now provide the written verbiage to send to these prospects. Remember to use your own name, address, and phone number.

CHAPTER 11

Marketing and Branding for Retirement Services

"The 401(k) Specialist" recently featured the retirement marketing presentations of RPAG partners Jason Caudle and Chip Morton. The article also addressed the topic of how retirement plan advisors look to promote and enhance their business opportunities when they favor referral partners who in turn are referred to them. Morton told attendees at a 401k Specialist Sales Strategies Conference in the Bahamas that, in a session aimed at what he calls "Power Marketing," retirement plan advisors should try various marketing strategies for attracting improved business opportunities as well as increased centers of influence.

In a podcast aimed at advisors and based on a presentation he co-delivered at the 2018 NAPA 401(k) Summit, Caudle enhanced his "Real Plan Advisors" marketing strategies to include ideas for use of robo-advisory services and setting up the staffing and technology to accommodate self-directed investment services. He also explained the similarities and differences between a CEFEX industry-recognized retirement plan advisor and the role of a "retirement services provider." Morton started two companies that help advisors promote their "retirement services provider" status in light of new technology such as robo-advisors that enable plan participants to work with an advisor on ways to create sustainable retirement income. Caudle, formerly a financial advisor, said "Guided Portfolios" at a retirement plan can be a "low maintenance upsell to create diversified income portfolios post-retirement." He now operates his own clearing firm. Both Morton's and Caudle's companies provide support exclusively to PlanAdviser of the Year candidates.

CHAPTER 12

Ethical Considerations in Retirement Planning

The role of the financial planner from an ethical perspective is two-fold. Planners perform both a navigational and an interpretative function. This chapter is premised on two assumptions. First, experts working in collaborative relationships with clients are required to assist them in navigating choices and options effectively. Second, they are required to assess potential outcomes and alternatives (thermal intelligence or interpretation). Several key aspects of the retirement planning environment are covered. There are distinct areas of ethical risk that arise in retirement planning that are not present in the pre-retirement phase. The ethical risks that confront retirement advisers are centred around issues such as withdrawals of superannuation, assignment of death benefits, safeguards for clients in superannuation withdrawal phase, training of staff to address retirement issues, practical ethical guidance in managing the various ethical decisions in retirement and the economic rational for focusing on ethical standards in retirement advice and counselling.

The importance of ethical issues in retirement planning. It is submitted that the ethical structure of the financial planning process is only efficacious in the retirement situation if professional standards address the retirement phase of client need as a discrete specialist area. Anecdotal evidence suggests that the retirement specialist with a thorough knowledge of the social effects of ageing and retirement and the numerous available health, housing, financial, legal and personal options is required when decision-making constraints are removed in a deregulated financial superannuation environment. Any professional financial planner who advises clients in any area of old age should be educated (by a competent body) on the rights and responsibilities which are part of the 'old age' package. It is presumable also considered the single most crucial reason that the adoption of a code of ethics and practice by the Executive Committee of the International Institute for Remuneration and Professional Practice and this code can act as a guide for financial planners worldwide.

CHAPTER 13

Case Studies and Best Practices

DelVecchio and Selbst provide insights from both successful and challenging scenarios. Pong presents a robo planner to engage clients, and Poerwanto's case study examines recommendations tailored to a client in the pre-retirement stage. Sidani discusses a planning process that identifies and mitigated client risks. Tollafield and Russo describe how firms can get multiple services for their clients, while Scigliano provides best practices for finding potential cross-sell partners. Covington presents the results of a study matching financial planning clients with non-client advisors representing various specialties and Blanchett and Watkins detail what distinguishes clients experiencing retirement hardships. Roche, Ireland, and Waples outline the top 10 practical takeaways for retirement planning from the Emerging Issues in Financial Planning 2021 research poster sessions and competition. And, in our last issue, Mosley shares best practices for marketing financial planning services to church congregations and Ligerud provides several ideas on how financial advisory firms might differentiate their services.

This instructional case is designed to be suitable for financial planning educators teaching a course on retirement planning. This case analysis focuses on goals and suitable investment recommendations for a nearly-retired client with a specific set of risks and preferences: Susan West, a new client with a retirement savings portfolio nearing $350,000. This personal saving is meant to produce passive retirement income as she phases into retirement in "a few years' time". In developing an investment recommendation, this case requires the student to identify some of Susan's areas of life where she is facing "lifestyle", "inflationary", and other "real-world" risks, then develop a corresponding set of strategies or adjustments to reduce vulnerabilities and improve outcomes.

CHAPTER 14

Conclusion and Future Trends

We began this essay by stating the background information of retirement and the retirement industry, outlined the history and journey of various theories, and then examined what retirement is and what the retiree may be looking for by retiring. We then looked at how psychological capital could link to retirement. We discussed what happened to people as they headed towards retirement, and the possible implications of any changes in what retirement was in the past and what retirement is now. Given its current nature, providing information on retirement planning, knowledge about the change in expertise, could prove helpful to retiree clients.

We focused primarily on what financial planners and financial planning clients may be seeing, hearing, and experiencing as they help clients through a critical phase of the financial planning process. We also looked at the particular issues identified by the financial planners that may affect their work in guiding clients to retirement. The issues identified by the financial planners were those that required a comprehensive view that depended on the financial planner's own degree of expertise. There is substantial evidence from this research to support a range of suggestions to aid financial planners in the next phase of financial planning. More research on this topic is certain to be published in the future, and we anticipate a move to involve the range of other services and professionals who clients would be expecting to visit as they head to retirement. This will be an important area of any further research in this particular series. Synthetic social concerns to the discussion. Research past retirement "exit" into the retirement "descent" phase would also be of particular interest. Ultimately, this move may help reduce or take action on any gaps in service to the client, providing a valuable focus to practice in their corporate social responsibility commitments in this area which in theory would directly benefit *some* older clients. Such work may also offer interesting insights into professionals looking at what the client will be doing after retirement. Again, however, other sectors remaining behind – what about the client who might work post-retirement?

www.ingramcontent.com/pod-product-compliance
Lightning Source LLC
Chambersburg PA
CBHW051504140726
47987CB00006B/2875